WAITING

How To Bloom Where You Are Planted

DEARAL L. JORDAN

WestBow
PRESS
A DIVISION OF THOMAS NELSON

ISBN: 978-1-4497-7583-4 (sc)
ISBN: 978-1-4497-7584-1 (e)

Library of Congress Control Number: 2012921411

WestBow Press books may be ordered through booksellers or by contacting:

WestBow Press
A Division of Thomas Nelson
1663 Liberty Drive
Bloomington, IN 47403
www.westbowpress.com
1-(866) 928-1240

Printed in the United States of America

WestBow Press rev. date: 12/5/2012

This book is dedicated to the Godhead; my wonderful, wife Denise; my sons, Dane and Tremaine; my mother, Eloise; my father, Elijah; and my pastor, Rev. James T. Meeks. I am the person that I am today because of them, and I thank God for blessing me with them each and every day.

Contents

Acknowledgments

To everyone who has inspired, prayed, encouraged, advised, helped, reviewed, corrected, suggested, and questioned this project, from my heart to yours, thank you. I have no idea how I could have completed this book without your involvement. I believe each one of you was placed in my life for a time such as this.

My prayer is that the Lord will bless you with others who will help you to fulfill the plans he has for your lives.

Introduction

This book is inspired by God to bring encouragement to anyone involved in situations where it seems difficult to move ahead. It is for anyone who feels the time has come to try something new because they are tired of the same day in and day out routine. In addition, it is for those who believe they can no longer stay in the present condition they find themselves in, whether a marriage, job, relationship, or ministry. If you find yourself in a rough or uncertain situation, it may be a lot like being planted in a flowerpot with nowhere to go. The best thing we can do for ourselves is to learn how to bloom where we are planted.

Waiting is a practical guide for anyone who wants to learn how to be content in their present situation or to make the best out of a bad situation. I will use my personal experiences to support my point of view and the Bible (NASB) to build my case as I uncover biblical principles on how one may bloom right where one is planted.

Looking back over my early years of ministry, I can honestly say that from time to time I felt as if the Lord was taking too long to move me into what I felt I should be doing. You see, I just believed that I was being held back from accomplishing or fulfilling the calling that was on my life, all because I wasn't good enough. Often I wondered why it seemed as if the Lord was passing me over and allowing other people around me to be all they could be. For a long time, I was a little upset with God.

Let's be honest for a moment. Haven't you felt that way at one time or another? You saw things as being unfair when it came to being promoted, acknowledged, or even given a chance to show that you were capable of doing the job better than someone else. This is one of the main reasons I wrote this book. I want to help you grow beyond feeling this way.

These feelings will bring about emotional distress that will destroy you if you allow it to. The emotions always seem to rise up at the very moment when you think you've overcome them. You see, these types of feelings are known as strongholds, which are designed to keep us in bondage. This is not a good place for any person to be as he or she seeks to please God on this journey.

When I look back on those moments, I wonder how I got past them. As believers, we can always refer to scriptures that relate to how we should handle things such as this, but for many, including myself, reading scripture did not always alleviate how I felt. As long as we are trapped within these physical bodies, certain feelings will continually try to rear their ugly heads. And when they do, we are to simply shift to another mindset. We must learn how to wait for God, and in our waiting, we must remember God's promises to us.

Sometimes the Lord will use people, things, methods, and right or wrong ways of doing things just so he can grow us up. The Lord wants to get us to a place where we no longer desire to be like someone else or to have done for us what he has done for others.

"For I know the plans that I have for you, declares the Lord, plans for welfare and not for calamity to give you a future and a hope" (Jeremiah 29:11 NASB). Looking back on everything I have experienced over the years, I realize it was all a part of the Lord's plan for me. Never once was the Lord out to get me, nor was he trying to keep me from doing or becoming what he had planned. Throughout all of this, the Lord our God was looking out for my well-being and my future. Not having any idea of what he was up to, I had to learn how to bloom where I had been planted. God expects for you and I to grow and expand in life wherever we may be planted at that present moment.

You may be in a relationship or marriage where you have lost interest and are torn between leaving and staying. Or you may have a job that you hate getting up every morning to go to because you believe you should be doing something else. Some of us are in ministries where we may feel as if everyone is being used by God except us, and it seems as if heaven has closed its mouth, God is not speaking, and we just don't know what we are supposed to do.

Before I move on, I am not endorsing or advocating that a person in an abusive marriage or relationship stay in that situation. This is not the will of God, and he is not asking you to stay in this type of environment so that you can grow. There is no place in the Bible or in a court of law that supports this type of behavior, and it can't be justified with the statement "for better or for worse" found in our vows. Being abusive toward others, regardless of its form, doesn't sit well with God.

There are some things in life for which we must accept the inevitable. On this journey, we will face situations that can't be avoided. To everyone in a difficult situation desperately trying to find their way out, there is a God who is able to bring you out, but we must learn how to wait. We need to come to the realization that sometimes the places we're in are the places we are supposed to be, and we may be there for a while. Since we are going to be there, we might as well learn how to grow where we are placed.

As we cover the principles found in Jeremiah 29:4–11(NASB) concerning how to bloom where we are planted and to wait for the Lord to fulfill his promises, we will discover how the children of Israel found themselves in a very difficult situation. They were in a place where they felt they didn't deserve to be, even though they had brought it upon themselves, just as so many of us have done. Do you recall what you may have done that contributed to where you are now, either good or bad? For others, we are where we are today because the Lord has placed us there. God knows the plans he has for us, and we must be prepared because our plans can change at any moment.

Chapter 1

How the Plans May Change

Upon leaving college, I had hopes of working as an artist for a major advertising firm. Instead, my first job out of college was as a shoe salesman. From the time I took that job to the time I left, I never once believed it was all I would end up becoming in life. However, part of learning how to bloom where you are planted starts with always keeping a positive attitude about the greatness that lies within you, and that greatness will never allow you to rest. You will always be in pursuit of that greatness until life itself ends.

After leaving the shoe business, I became a sales rep for a major carpet company. From 1980 to 1986, I worked my way up to an assistant manager position and was working toward managing my own store one day. One particular evening, the woman who would eventually become my wife, whom I am still happily married to, came into the store to purchase carpet. There was just something different about her. I can't

1

quite remember how we began to talk about maybe going out so we could get to know each other better, but now she is my wife and we have been together since 1987. The Lord was orchestrating the entire plan he had for my life.

I had no idea that God had a plan for me to become an ordained minister, licensed to preach the gospel. The Lord reminds us, and his prophet in Jeremiah 1:5 (NASB), that he knew us before he formed us in our mother's womb. And before we were born, he had already set us aside for something special. The one thing that has kept me all these years it is knowing that the Lord has selected me for greatness and that it shall come to pass. Not only has he selected me, but you also have been selected to do something great as well.

After we got married in 1987, I left my job as an assistant manager. At the time, I just wanted to serve in full-time ministry. However, I was unable to find full-time employment. Things became really bad, but I would never give up believing that God had something better for us. Eventually I was offered a position in full-time ministry. To date, I have served in ministry for over twenty years, and I shall continue to serve in this capacity *until the Lord moves me*. When I think back on how I got to this point in life, I have to ask myself several questions: What if I had not met my wife as I did, or what if I had decided to leave ministry because of just wanting to do something else?

This is where many of us are today in life; we want to leave because things are not going as we planned. This is a very difficult place for anyone to be. Many of us think to ourselves, *if only I could move to some place other than where I am now.* The problem most of us face when we are in these situations is not having any place to go or any idea as to what we should do. However, even with this, if we would plan to stay where we are until something better comes along, or until the Lord moves us, we could truly bloom where God has planted us.

In the proceeding chapters, I hope to offer you sound advice to aid you in blooming where the Lord has planted you, with the thought of acceptance leading the way.

Chapter 1 Reflection:

_____

_____

_____

_____

_____

_____

_____

_____

_____

_____

_____

_____

_____

_____

_____

_____

Chapter 2

How to Accept Where You Are

"Thus says the Lord of hosts, the God of Israel, to all the exiles whom I have sent into exile from Jerusalem to Babylon" (Jeremiah 29:4 NASB). This text clearly shows that the God of Israel had everything to do with sending the children of Israel into captivity because of their constant disobedience. He placed them there to show them that there were consequences for their actions. If we are going to bloom where we are planted, we must first accept that God has placed us where we are for a season and that sometimes he allows us to be where we are because of something we ourselves have caused.

We should also keep in mind that God knows where we are, and he knows everything about the conditions we're in. Even if we had something to do with where we are today, we must remember that the Lord may just decide to keep us there for a set period of time. Once we accept that God has placed us where we are, we can live on the promise that he knows the plans for our lives, and it is working together for our good.

The person who placed the seeds in the pot of a certain plant I received as a gift knew the potential of the seeds that were planted. If the seeds were planted in the right soil and properly tended to, the seeds would have the chance of growing into a beautiful and healthy plant. Just like that plant, being in ministry all these years has helped me to discover my potential and who I really am. I have found out things about myself that I had no idea even existed. Every assignment, project, meeting, shifting, moving, mistake, and situation that I was placed in was the right soil for me, and God has been tending that soil for all of these years. Not only have I seen my growth, but through time, others have seen it as well.

Once I realized what the Lord had given me, I knew that the gates of hell could not put a stop to what God had planned for me. And the same is true for you. No matter how bad it may have been or how great the pressure was, I knew that I would one day overcome, and that day is now. Even today the Lord is still doing a little pruning and digging on me. Because he knows there is more that lies within, and I have more growing up to do. The growing process for us as believers never stops.

We are all seeds planted by God, placed in certain situations for a specific period of time because he knows the potential of what lies within us, and he is trying to bring all of that out so that we can be used to bring glory to him. If we refuse to accept that God has placed us where we are for a reason and refuse to bloom where we have been planted, not only are we letting the Lord down, we are also doing an injustice to ourselves and others.

Wherever God places us, he knows how much we can bear. Most of us have heard that the Lord will never put more upon us than we can bear; this is a promise made to us by God. Every time I thought I could not take any more of what I felt, God already knew that I could take a little more, and he was not going to allow me to give up on becoming everything he had planned for me to become. Through this process, I have learned that we all bear things differently and the results are different as well. Our situations are tailor-made specifically for the sole purpose of developing us into the best we can become.

Not all plants were made to bloom or grow in all conditions, just as we all were not made to grow in the same situations. But God, who knows where we can grow, has arranged for us to be right where we are for that specific reason. God is not in the business of keeping us from growing. However, he *is* in the business of maturing us as believers.

I know you may want to get out or run away from your present situation, but just as plants are moved to larger pots when they have outgrown the pot they were originally planted in, the Lord may not move us or change some of the situations we find ourselves in, until we show some signs of growth. Until this takes place, we may as well get comfortable in those places.

Chapter 2 Reflection:

_____

_____

_____

_____

_____

_____

_____

_____

_____

_____

_____

_____

_____

_____

_____

Chapter 3

How to Get Comfortable

"Build houses and *live in them*; and plant gardens and eat their produce" (Jeremiah 29:5 NASB). If we are to bloom where we are planted, the next thing we must do is learn to be content with where we are. We have to decide to make the best of whatever situation we find ourselves in because we will be there for an undetermined period of time.

God told the children of Israel to build houses and plant gardens because they were going to be where they were for at least seventy years—a long time to be around people you are in bondage to; nevertheless, even in this, God wanted them to be comfortable. Moreover, the same people the Israelites were in bondage to would ultimately play a significant role in bringing forth the plan God had for their lives.

Becoming comfortable doesn't mean we should become complacent. At times, we may find ourselves in very uncomfortable situations where we want out as soon as possible, but God wants us to learn how to wait for him. This waiting period should be viewed as a time of preparation. During this period, God is strengthening our faith and forcing us to depend totally upon him. When we see things in this light, we are more apt to relax and enjoy the journey. In the past, I was unable to see God in my situations. I found it difficult to find rest and to believe that this was his way of preparing me for the place he was taking me to— my next level of spiritual maturity.

Wherever you may find yourself at this moment, it is important that you build yourself up. If we are to build ourselves up to become comfortable where we are planted, we must start with the foundation, Jesus Christ.

Without him, no building can take place; neither can comfort or growth. Jesus Himself says, "I am the vine, you are the branches; he who abides in Me and I in him, he bears much fruit, for apart from Me you can do nothing" (John 15:5 NASB).

If you have never invited Jesus into your heart to become your Lord and Savior, I encourage you to stop and take a moment to do just that. It is the only way for you and I to abide in him, and he in us. We must believe that he is God's only begotten son. He came to save us from our sins and destruction, and only through him can you and I inherit eternal life. If you believe this, I ask that you would pray this prayer to invite him in: *Lord Jesus, I am a sinner who wishes to change my life. I ask for forgiveness of my sins and desire to turn from my wicked ways. I accept the truth about who you are and what you did for me. Please come into my life as my Lord and Savior. Amen.* "Whoever will call on the name of the Lord will be saved" (Romans 10:13 NASB). Congratulations, you are now a child of God and you have become a part of his kingdom. Now it is time for you to bloom where you are planted. Not only do we receive the promise of eternal life, but we also receive the promise of the Holy Spirit according to John 14:16 (NASB). This is very important to know because if we are going to bloom where we are planted, we can be assured that we have help on our side to make it happen.

As Jesus explained in Matthew 7:24 (NASB), a person who builds his or her life on him is as wise as the man who built his house on a rock instead of sand. The man clearly understood that storms would rise and strong winds would blow, and if there were any chance for his home to remain intact, he would have to build his house on something more solid. The same is true for anyone who has hopes of surviving life's storms as they arise in the midst of our growing and seasons of preparation. This is when storms will enter into our lives the most, only to prove that with Christ we have become more than conquerors.

If I had decided to build myself on anything other than Jesus Christ, I know that I would not have survived. Praise God for his son in whom I encourage you to build everything upon.

After the Lord instructed the Israelites to build houses in which to live and raise their families, he also told them to plant gardens. Why is this so significant? Simply because planting gardens would play a major role in reminding them that many seasons would come and go during their time of exile. By planting the right seeds at the right time, they could expect the harvest to bring forth much fruit.

To bloom where we are planted, we must realize that, "There is an appointed time for everything. And there is a time for every event under heaven-------A time to give birth and a time to die; A time to plant and a time to uproot what is planted." (Ecclesiastes 3:1–2 NASB). Wherever you may be on this journey of life, just remember that our lives are full of seasons that will come and go, and that each season comes with its own personal purpose. During seasons of planting, we must be careful of the seeds we plant at that time.

Whatever you do, *never* plant seeds of complaint while waiting on God. Complaining while in the midst of blooming where you are planted will always lead to disappointment, and it may cause you to miss the blessings of God for your life. Planting seeds of complaint keeps us from moving forward, and it overshadows whatever faith we may have in God. When your faith is blinded by complaining, you can easily begin to believe that things will never change.

I personally remember how I felt when I sowed seeds of complaint. Honestly, I felt real good about it until I realized that it was evolving into something much stronger and more dangerous. My complaining was gaining momentum because I was connecting to others who had the same spirit and mind-set as I did. The complaining developed into tearing things down, which led to my morale decreasing. Ministry no longer was enjoyable or meaningful; it had become a challenge, and that was not good.

As I saw myself changing, I also no longer felt the joy I used to have in serving others. When I noticed that everything God had planned for me was slowly slipping away right before my eyes, I knew that I had to get back on track immediately. After being whipped by the Holy Spirit about how this was not part of the growing process, I repented and the Lord restored me. Now, when my flesh wants to complain, the Spirit of the Lord reminds me that I should pray instead.

If you have planted seeds of complaint, you must pluck those seeds up if you plan to bloom where you are planted. Becoming comfortable with where you are and planting the right seeds will always lead to reproduction.

Chapter 3 Reflection:

_____

_____

_____

_____

_____

_____

_____

_____

_____

_____

_____

_____

_____

_____

_____

_____

Chapter 4

How to Reproduce Yourself

"Take wives and become the fathers of sons and daughters, and take wives for your sons and give your daughters to husbands, that they may bear sons and daughters; and multiply there and do not decrease"(Jeremiah 29:6 NASB). The overall theme that runs through this verse is increase. God knew this could only be done if the children of Israel were consistent in reproducing, so he encouraged them to take wives for themselves, wives for their sons, and to give their daughters to husbands so that they could have many children. By doing so, they would never have to worry about becoming extinct. Remember, they were destined to be in captivity for seventy years, and generations would come and go over time.

While we're waiting on God to promote, elevate, or move us, we must learn how to reproduce where we are at the present time. If we are not blooming, growing, or increasing in size, why would there be a reason for us to be moved, or have expectations that things will change?

When I took a closer look at the plastic pot in which the plant had been planted in that I mentioned earlier, I discovered that the pot was expanding because the plant was reproducing itself, and it needed more room to grow. It was reshaping where it had been planted. If the plant had any hope of surviving, I would have to replant it to a larger pot. If I did not move it to a larger pot, it would eventually die.

The Lord wants to move you to a bigger pot. Remember the Lord's plan for our lives is to prosper us and not to harm us. It's his desire for us to live and not die. If you're in a tough spot in your marriage, your ministry, or on your job, you need to reshape the pot that you are presently in by reproducing yourself skillfully and spiritually, and seek to become the best that you can in God's eyes. When this takes place, the Lord will move us to a bigger pot, or place us in a better situation where we can continue to grow for his glory. If we don't do so, we can't expect to be moved to another level on our spiritual journey.

We could only accomplish this by learning all there is to learn about where we may be presently. When we learn all we can about our jobs, relationships, ministries, or positions, and apply these skills to what we do in order to become the best, we are making ourselves anew. Consequently, the pot we are planted in seemingly decreases, as we expand and grow. From reading a book to taking a class, you should do whatever it takes for you to reproduce yourself.

To everyone who has graduated with a degree and still unable to find a job in your field of interest, don't get discouraged. For whatever job you are able to obtain, just work hard at becoming the best even if you think it's a position below your standards. Avoid grumbling and becoming upset or mad with God and others. Realize what God is doing for you. He is growing you up so that he can eventually move you to a better situation. We also reproduce ourselves when we decide to pour into others, as someone has poured into us. Kingdom building is all about growing up the body of Christ. In whom are you planting seeds, and what type of seeds are they?

God wants us to continue to grow in Christ on a daily basis as well. Often we are placed where we are by God so that we can mature spiritually. When we find ourselves questioning God, asking: *Why am I in this marriage? Why do you have me on this job knowing that I can't stand the people I work with or work for? Why do you have me in this church, when everyone in the ministry is out to get me? Why?* Trust what I am about to say: the Lord is bringing the best out of you.

He wants us to reproduce ourselves spiritually in Jesus. When we find ourselves planted in him, this is accomplished. "Abide in Me, and I in you. As the branch cannot bear fruit of itself unless it abides in the vine, so neither can you unless you abide in Me. I am the vine, you are the branches; he who abides in Me and I in him, he bears much fruit, for apart from Me you can do nothing. My Father is glorified by this, that you bear much fruit" (John 15:4–5, 8 NASB). If we desire to glorify our heavenly Father in our lives regardless of where we are presently, we must be connected to Christ. A proper connection to him will bring forth a fruitful and abundant life that matures us as believers.

God will use our particular situation for a certain period of time to grow us up. One reason why so many believers are still at the level they were when they got saved is because they are not producing any fruit spiritually. Producing where we are planted starts with Christ. We must produce the right type of fruit, if we are to have any hope of maturing in Christ. According to Galatians 5: 22–24 (NASB), as believers we should be only bearing this type of fruit, love, joy, peace, patience, kindness, goodness, faithfulness, gentleness, and self-control.

Why must we bear this type of fruit in the conditions in which we find ourselves? Bearing this type of fruit before others gives them the opportunity to see what God is like. If we are not producing fruit in our lives, we are not blooming in God's eyes. If we are not blooming, we can't expect any type of change in our condition.

Even though I know there are many testimonies out there regarding this issue of bearing the right type of fruit for others, and it would take a while to gather some of them, I would love to present myself as exhibit A. While on this journey, I have discovered how powerful and impactful this process of bearing fruit can be. When I decided to give the Word of God a try instead of waiting for others to change, I made up my mind to change myself. And when I did, those whom were once viewed as my enemies, whom may still be my enemies, they began to change how they treated me, without understanding why.

Planting the seeds of abiding in Jesus will always produce fruit, which will not only change our lives, but it will also change the lives of those around us. The fruit that comes from having a right relationship with Jesus causes one to see others as God sees them. The Lord also knows what is missing in their lives, and he wants to use us to bring this revelation to the forefront of their lives.

If a person is able to discover the true nature of God, that person's life can be changed for eternity. This is why we are placed in certain places for a certain period of time. Not only is the Lord working on us, but he is working on those around us as well. Just as he has a plan for our lives, he has a plan for them as well. Often, we are both a part of each other's plan.

Displaying this type of reproduction where we are planted, toward those with whom we may live, work, or serve, leaves the impression that not only does God care about them; but also we do too. The Lord wants each of us to recognize and participate in his overall plan for mankind. Isn't it something how the Lord can use imperfect people such as you and me to reach others on his behalf? We just need to make ourselves anew in Jesus. In order to bloom where we are planted, it's imperative that we also care about those around us. Regardless of how they may treat us, we must be truly concerned about their welfare.

Chapter 4 Reflection:

_____

_____

_____

_____

_____

_____

_____

_____

_____

_____

_____

_____

_____

_____

_____

_____

Chapter 5

How to Care For Others

"Seek the welfare of the city where I have sent you into exile, and pray to the Lord on its behalf; for in its welfare you will have welfare" (Jeremiah 29:7 NASB). As we continue to pursue how to bloom where we are planted, we must understand that if God has anything to do with it, we will be challenged to do some unexpected things. His ways are not our ways and he does not think as we think. By taking a closer look at this verse, we will discover how we can be blessed in a rough situation, or in a place we don't want to be, just by caring for someone else's welfare.

In this verse, the word *welfare* means *peace*. So, if we want to have peace in the places where there is no peace for us, we must first learn how to pray for the welfare of others. God gives the children of Israel a charge that seems to be a little backwards. He tells them to seek peace and prosperity for their enemies. As if that wasn't enough, he wants them to pray for them as well. I could only imagine how the children of God wanted to respond to this request. It would probably sound like this: "Lord, have you forgotten that these people are our enemies? Instead of praying for them and wishing that they prosper, we should be praying for their destruction and our release. How about giving us permission to tear them down with our words, or to do something to harm them?"

How does all of this fit for those of us who find ourselves in relationships gone sour, on jobs we dislike, or in ministries where we view people around us as being our enemies? Remember, the Lord our God knows the plans he has for our lives. Once we understand that blooming where we are planted has nothing to do with us, but it has everything to do with what the Lord wants, then we can be open to whatever the Lord may request of us as we seek to grow.

If we are going to grow where we are, not only are we to love our enemies with the love of Christ, but we are also to be concerned about their well-being. I know you are probably saying, "You don't know my spouse, ministry leader, or boss as I do." You are right, I don't know them, but God does and he knows that whatsoever we plant, we shall also reap. If we plant prayers of peace and prosperity for them, the God we serve will see to it that the same is returned to us.

We are admonished in Matthew 5:44 (KJV): To love our enemies, bless them that curse us, do good to them that hate us, and pray for them which despitefully use and persecute us. This is a commandment given to all believers by Jesus, and when we choose not to follow what he has told us to, we continue to live unproductive lives as we are committing a sin. Sin will not only hinder our prayers, but it will also keep God from blessing us, as he desires to. According to verse 45, if we want to be considered as sons and daughters of God, we must conduct ourselves as children of our heavenly Father. And as children of God we are to love our enemies.

The people around us whom may hope the worst for us have lives filled with unrest. This may be the reason why they treat you and me as they do. But when we seek peace for them through our prayers and our actions, we receive peace in return. First Corinthians 14:33 (NASB) proves that God is not the author of confusion, conflict, or things being out of order, but he is the God of peace. So, as we extend peace unto others, we are sharing with them the peace of God. Not only are we to pray that they have peace in their lives, but it would also help if we would pray for them to prosper in their lives.

Along with prayer, we can also do something to show them how concerned we are about them. We can accomplish this by simply asking them, "What can I do for you to help you to be successful, or how can I help you to get what you need to get done?" By putting aside our own agendas and picking up theirs, we are creating a favorable atmosphere that will produce rewarding results for the kingdom of God. Just try it, and if it doesn't work, you are welcome to go back to the old you.

When we come to people with a sincere concern for them, it catches them off guard. They have no idea how to accept it because they are not used to having someone extend genuine love to them. In our own walks, we may encounter times when things don't seem to be working in our favor and some situations just seem unproductive. This is primarily because we have decided to deal with people as we think they should be dealt with and not how God has told us to deal with them.

As we continue to seek ways by which we may grow and develop into everything the Lord has planned for us, we must be careful about how we receive the things we hear regarding the plans that God has for us.

Chapter 5 Reflection:

_____

_____

_____

_____

_____

_____

_____

_____

_____

_____

_____

_____

_____

_____

_____

_____

Chapter 6

How to Listen to God

"For thus says the Lord of host, the God of Israel, Do not let your prophets who are in your midst and your diviners deceive you, and do not listen to the dreams which they dream. For they prophesy falsely to you in My name; I have not sent them; declares the Lord" (Jeremiah 29: 8–9 NASB). God gave this message to the Israelites because the prophets who were among them were liars. They lied so well that they convinced the leaders to believe that the Lord had spoken to them. Some would agree that the false prophets were the major cause of the captivity of the Israelites.

God knows there will be people around us whom will have their own opinions or thoughts about where we should be and what we should be doing regarding our present condition. Some will even claim that they have heard from the Lord on your behalf. They mean well, but we must be very careful in accepting what they have to say. We must learn to hear the voice of God for ourselves if we are going to bloom where we are planted. We are not to listen to those who have no idea as to what the Lord has told us. Stay away from those who claim they have a word from God for you. If what they have to say does not line up with what you have heard from the Lord yourself, you need to get away from them quickly.

The Lord had already told the Israelites how long they would be in captivity, but the prophets claimed that they instead had the right time for their release. If the truth be told, how many of us have ever gotten a date from God regarding our release or change? They even spoke of the dreams that the Lord had given them regarding their captivity. The Lord made it very clear that he had not sent them, and he charged the people not to listen to them.

In order to hear what the Lord has to say regarding where we are and whether it is time to leave or stay, we must have our own, personal relationship with him. This relationship can only develop to the point where we are able to clearly hear the voice of God versus the voice of self, or Satan, by spending quality time with him. The more time we spend with God in prayer, reading his Word and regularly attending church, the easier it becomes for us to hear him clearly. From Moses to Paul, we can find a common thread regarding how the Lord personally spoke to those for whom he had specific plans. Even if there were others around them, these individuals were always able to hear God for themselves.

Moving before our time, all because of what someone else may feel or think they heard, could cause us to miss everything the Lord may have for us. I know many people who moved before it was time to move, all because they listened to others. Now they are working harder to make things happen on their own. I am not saying that things will be easier for those of us who hear God and decide to follow him, but I do believe being obedient to the voice of God brings greater satisfaction.

People would come to me all of the time saying things like, "Rev. Jordan, the Lord is getting ready to move you. He told me to tell you that it will not be long because he has bigger things for you. Just get ready, because he is getting ready to take you to the next level." All of this may have even been true, but I would have to be sure it was the Lord who was speaking and not others, just as in Judges 6:17(NASB). Gideon asked the Lord for a sign to be sure it was he who was talking. I myself have asked the Lord to give me a sign on many occasions.

To avoid missing the time of our release, you have to learn how to ask for signs as well. There are three things you must possess if you have hopes of getting a sign from the Lord. First, you must be faithful to God and to the task that is already before you. Second, you must be covered with humility and recognize that you are nothing without God. Finally, you must be willing to give or sacrifice the most important thing you have, which is yourself, unto the Lord.

I am not sure how the Lord will speak, nor do I know when he shall speak. However, there is one thing I do know, and that is this: the Lord is not a God of confusion. When it's time for the Lord to move us by speaking to us, we will not have to second-guess whether or not he is speaking.

Most of us have heard from the Lord, but we have yet to move into what he has called us to. Why? Could it be that we are afraid of the unknown, and we have no idea what we are to do when we get there? Could it be that we have become too attached to where we are? This bond or tie we have with where we are becomes very difficult to break because, we feel that we would be letting someone down if we left them. Most of us have become so comfortable with where we are that it doesn't take a lot of dependence on God anymore.

We feel secure financially, we don't worry about being challenged, and there is no desire to break the day-to-day routine. Not taking that step can also cause us to miss whatever the Lord has for us. This type of response made to God's spoken word regarding our lives says a lot about our faith in him. We will cover this a bit more in chapter 8.

I am more than sure that when he is ready to tell us, God is capable of letting us know what he wants us to know. Then, he will send others to confirm it. While waiting on the Lord to speak, we must learn how to keep the promises he has made to us.

Chapter 6 Reflection:

Chapter 7

How to Keep His Promise

"For thus says the Lord, When seventy years have been completed for Babylon, I will visit you and fulfill My good word to you to bring you back to this place" (Jeremiah 29:10 NASB). God says when your time is up you will know; this is why we must only listen to him and no one else. He assured the children of Israel that he was the only one who knew the plans he had for them.

The promise that the Lord made to the children of Israel was this: at the end of the seventy years of captivity, he would personally visit them and fulfill the promise of returning them back to the place that belonged to them. They would not return as slaves but as inheritors of the land promised to them.

We may not have been given a timeline as to when our situations may change, but if we believe that the Lord is the one who sets the time, we must also believe that he will show up at the right time to restore us to the promises he has given us. As believers, all we have are the promises of God. He is not a man, and it is impossible for him to lie. If you really think about it, has there ever been a time that he hasn't come through on your behalf? The old folks would say, "He may not come when you want him, but he's always right on time."

According to everything the Lord has promised to his children, not one word has failed. And we can find every promise he has made to his children throughout the entire Bible. I would like to encourage you to seek out those promises, so that you can experience the fullness of God for yourself. Because of God's glory and excellence, we have received his great and precious promises. His promises are trustworthy because he is faithful.

Do you know the promise that the Lord has made to you? If you know what that promise is, hold on to it. As long as you hold on to it, it will help you along the way, as you seek to bloom where you are planted. When you become sidetracked and discouraged, grab hold to the promise. Memorize it or write it down someplace where you can easily get to it. When you find yourself in those moments where you feel like you can't take anymore, and you feel like giving up, go back to the promise. Because I have experienced it for myself, trust me with what I am about to say: the promise that God has made to you will always bring you comfort and reassurance.

Not only did God promise to bring the children of Israel back to where he had promised them, but he also made an even greater promise to both them and everyone who believed.

That promise was Jesus Christ. Today, we have the privilege of experiencing the ultimate promise. If you did not know that you had a promise from God, this is it! The Savior of our souls who grants us eternal life, he has come as was promised in Isaiah 42:1–7 (NASB). If no other promise has manifested, just know this one has been fulfilled. This is where we all can hang our faith on.

For many, waiting on the Lord to perform what he has promised is where most of the problems lie. We grow tired of ministry, tired of people and their incompetence, tired of no change, and tired of work, as nothing seems to be going right with the boss. However, we should be encouraged by the fact that the Lord knows the set date and time when he will show up and change our situation. Learning how to bloom where we are planted teaches us to wait for God, and that's a promise.

So many people have left their situations before the appointed time. They could not wait, and now they are worse off than they were before. Moving too soon and not knowing where you are going or what you will do when you get there, can cause major setbacks regarding your growth if you don't know how to hold on to the promise.

People who are placed in situations not beneficial to their growth die spiritually, all because they have no promise from God to hold onto. But with a promise we are able to move forward.

Chapter 7 Reflection:

_____

_____

_____

_____

_____

_____

_____

_____

_____

_____

_____

_____

_____

_____

Chapter 8

How to Move Forward

As we continue to wait while we are growing, we are also developing a much closer relationship with the Lord Himself. If we follow the steps laid out before us, not only will the Lord fulfill every promise he has made to us, but he will also make known what that relationship will look like in the near future.

The passage of scripture found in Jeremiah 29:4–11(NASB) that I have covered throughout the book not only covers what to do when we are faced with certain situations, but it also deals with repentance that took place during the children of Israel's captivity. When following the Lord's plans for our lives in moments of despair, non-productivity, and bondage, or when we are just fed up with where we may be, something else takes place during the process known as going to the Lord and asking for his forgiveness.

Unfortunately, the children of Israel never got this

revelation, and they missed everything that the Lord had for them. As we learn to bloom where we're planted, we're also learning how to repent at different levels. True repentance on our part always sets the stage for God to draw closer to us, and us to him. When this type of relationship is established between God and us, then we are able to see our own spiritual growth in the Lord, and we are ready to move forward.

If you have not been moved or things have not changed regarding your situation, just hang in there. The Lord is getting everything ready for you. While waiting, you might as well ask God for forgiveness for the things you did wrong while you were going through, and reassure him that you have learned your lesson.

Not everyone always feels as if they are ready to move when the Lord is ready to move them. Often it starts from being fearful of the unknown. We all may say when the time comes for us to move, we will be ready, but most of us are not. If the Lord is ready to move you, you are more than ready to be moved. What happens is we begin to make up stories within ourselves that are full of what-ifs. What if it doesn't work out as I planned, What if the money is not there, What if they don't like me, What if I don't do well, or What if the Lord did not tell me to move?

I remember a few years back when I heard God clearly say to me, "Now is the time for you to go back to school to get your masters." It was during a long December vacation while at home in prayer. If you don't want to hear from God, just stay off your knees. When I heard him, it was as if he was physically right there in the room with me. There was no doubt in my mind that I had heard the Lord tell me that it was time for me to move. Even though I knew it was him talking, at that very moment my mind shifted in another direction.

I began to question myself. "Am I smart enough to enter seminary at this stage in my life? How am I going to pay for school if I get in? I know that I am not going to get in, so why should I even apply?" It took a while before I even contacted the school, because the "what-if" monster had risen. Finally, I applied because there was no peace to be found within. And within three weeks of submitting all of the necessary paperwork, I received my letter of acceptance to North Park Theological Seminary's Master of Divinity Program, even though it may take some time before I am finished. So far, the Lord has worked it out financially, and I have kept an overall 3.0 grade point average. And I thought that I was not smart enough. When the Lord says go, it is time to go.

Not moving when it is time to move only prolongs the plans that the Lord has for us and the opportunity to grow into everything God intends for us to become and do for his glory. Here you have been praying, fasting, and pleading for God to move and all you can say is, "I just want to be sure it is time." But on the other hand we have seen God move when we have moved on smaller scales. Things just came together as we stepped out on faith. Now we are faced with a major move, but we want to wait.

Sometimes we find ourselves waiting on God to move, when the Lord is waiting on us. Has he told you to go, as he spoke to Abraham when he wanted to use him to be a blessing to the world? He simply told Abraham to leave not only what he was attached to, which was his family, but the Lord also instructed him to leave his place of comfort and security. He went on to tell Abraham that he was sending him to a place where everything would be new to him, and he would have to rely totally on God in order to make it.

What about the story of how Peter walked on water? Was it about Peter having the ability to walk on water, or was it about him stepping out on faith to get to where the Lord was? Remember, Peter never stepped out on the water until the Lord bid him to come, and Peter was not going out there until he was sure that it was Jesus who was out there on the water doing the calling.

If he has spoken to you in this manner, don't blow it as so many others have done, including myself. Missing those moments at their appointed time will determine how soon you will get to where the Lord is moving you to. If you miss it, I would like to believe that the Lord will present the opportunity to you again. And if the Lord presents you with another chance just run with it.

Wherever the Lord may be sending or calling us to, it will be a place where we can grow to totally depend on him, and where we will be able to do greater things for the Lord. When I say greater things, I mean things that we have never done before. Even though what we believe the Lord has revealed to us about what we should be doing in the future may not take place as soon as we would like it to happen, I would like to leave you with this note: wait for the Lord, and learn how to bloom where you are planted.

Chapter 8 Reflection:

_____

_____

_____

_____

_____

_____

_____

_____

_____

_____

_____

_____

_____

_____

_____

Conclusion

Do you want to grow, mature, or be used by God? Then you must be connected to the main vine. Without that relationship, we can't be comfortable where we are. We will not find ourselves praying for others, and we are not going to be patient enough to wait for God as we should. Only in him can we find the strength we need to do what God is calling us to do.

"For I know the plans that I have for you, declares the Lord, plans for welfare and not calamity to give you a future and a hope." (Jeremiah 29:11 NASB). We must understand that God's thoughts are not like our thoughts. His way of thinking has everything to do with continually bringing him glory, and we are the beneficiaries of the outcome of those thoughts. Put another way, God knows everything there is to know about each one of us who belongs to him. He also knows everything there is to know about those who do not.

Knowing everything about us gives him the ability to know not only what we need, but also what is best for us. He has laid out plans that span from the beginning to the end of our lives. His plans for our lives are so well thought out that there should not be any concerns about what will become of us in the end.

God's thoughts for his people have always been and will

always be the same until the end of time. When we get to heaven, we shall experience the ultimate plan together with him. The Lord's thoughts for his people are that the day will come when they will be totally restored to him. Even though we may find ourselves in some tough situations at this present moment or even in the near future, we must realize that life on this side will have its ups and downs, but the plan is to get us to the place where peace will be around us at all times. Thank God for your difficult times because in them you get a chance to experience the peace of God, as you are assured of the fact that the day shall come where his peace in your life will never end.

When we find ourselves in moments of unrest, or even in places where we feel as if we are not growing or becoming everything we believe we are to be, the Lord is not sitting around thinking about how to bring harm to us, he is thinking about how to bring peace to that situation for us. This is how he always thinks. He changes not.

The Lord our God has a future for his people. Yes, there is more that the Lord has for us right at this very moment, and for the near future. These things he has for us will bring us peace, joy, contentment, and rest, as well as spiritual blessings that will be waiting for us in the near future. Praise the Lord!

The future that the Lord has consistently on his mind, and that he plans to give us, is a future of hope. (Jeremiah 17:7 NASB) states, "Blessed is the one who trusts in the Lord And whose trust is in the Lord." For everyone who places their faith, belief, and hope in the Lord is blessed with God's favor regardless of their situations. We have often placed our hope in everything except Jesus Christ. When we place our hope in him, we will be like a tree that has been planted by a river. In the context of the scripture passage, the word *planted* means *transplanted*. In Christ, we have been uprooted out of sin and transplanted into righteousness. We have been uprooted out of darkness and transplanted into the marvelous light. We have been uprooted from a place where sin was in control and transplanted to where sin no longer has power over us. We have been uprooted out of death into eternal life. This is the future hope that awaits us; just by knowing this, we can face whatever situations we may find ourselves in.

By staying put until he is ready to move us or change our present condition, we allow him to do all he wants to do through us in order to prepare us for our future.

As we grow where we are planted, we learn how to totally depend on God. Totally depending on the Lord places us in a position of complete submission. Submission at this degree allows us to accept that God has placed us where we are so we are able to find total contentment in reproducing ourselves.

This type of submission to God moves us to seek peace for others and to pray for their well-being. It also keeps us from listening to the wrong things as we learn how to wait. This is how we shall learn how to bloom where we are planted as we wait on God.